LIFE

Eating

By Holly Duhig

BookLife
PUBLISHING

©2019
BookLife Publishing
King's Lynn
Norfolk PE30 4LS

A catalogue record for this book is available from the British Library.

ISBN: 978-1-78637-441-7

Written by:
Holly Duhig

Edited by:
John Wood

Designed by:
Jasmine Pointer

Photocredits:
Images are courtesy of Shutterstock.com. With thanks to Getty Images, Thinkstock Photo and iStockphoto.

Front cover – Hogan Imaging. 2 – stock_shot. 3 – Hogan Imaging. 4 – Valentina Razumova, Susan Schmitz, Eric Isselee, Serhiy Kobyakov. 5 – Teerasak Ladnongkhun. 6 – Vecton, Miss Ty. 7 – Evgeniya L, Nolte Lourens, LightField Studios. 8 – Jen Watson. 9 – janaph, photomaster, LittlePerfectStock, Eric Isselee. 10 – Fer Gregory. 11 – Four Oaks, Ondrej Prosicky. 12 – Ramon Carretero. 13 – Martin Prochazkacz. 14 – Anton_Ivanov. 15 – Butterfly Hunter. 16 – Beatrice Prezzemoli. 17 – Cathy Keifer. 18 – Niney Azman. 19 – Alexlky. 20 – Greg Brave. 21 – Cornel Constantin 22 – wavebreakmedia. 23 – ifong.

Contents

Words that look like **this** can be found in the glossary on page 24.

What Is a Living Thing?

A living thing is something that is 'alive'. Humans are living things; so are cats, dogs, birds and fish. There are certain **processes** that make something a living thing. These are:

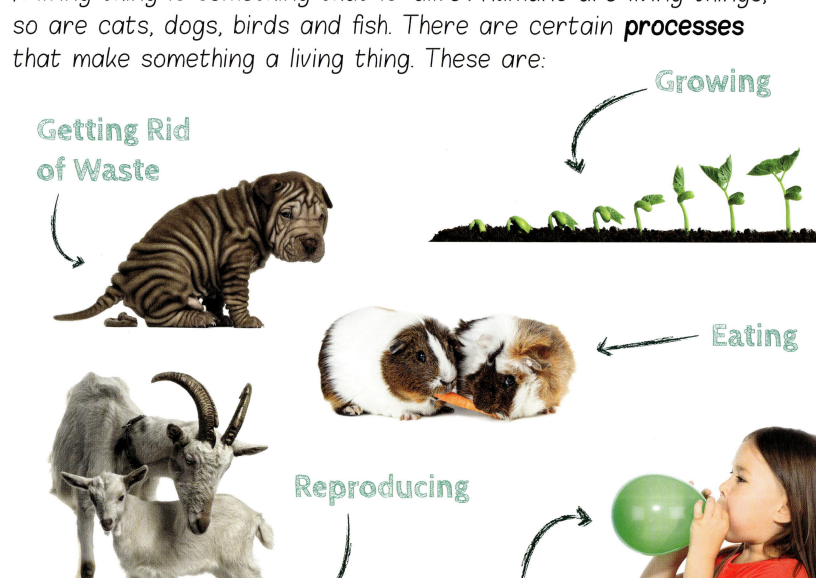

Growing

Getting Rid
of Waste

Eating

Reproducing

Breathing

Some things,
such as metal,
plastic and rocks,
have never
been alive.

Some things used to be alive but are now dead. The bones you give your dog, the brown leaves in autumn and the wood that makes your furniture were all parts of living things that are now dead.

What Is Eating?

Eating is the process of taking in food for energy. All living things need to eat to stay alive and healthy. Living things have many different body parts that help with eating, such as mouths and stomachs.

Mouth

Stomach

We can group living things together by the things they eat.

Herbivore

Living things that only eat plants are called herbivores.

Living things that only eat other animals are called carnivores.

Carnivore

Omnivore

Living things that eat plants and animals are called omnivores.

Mammals

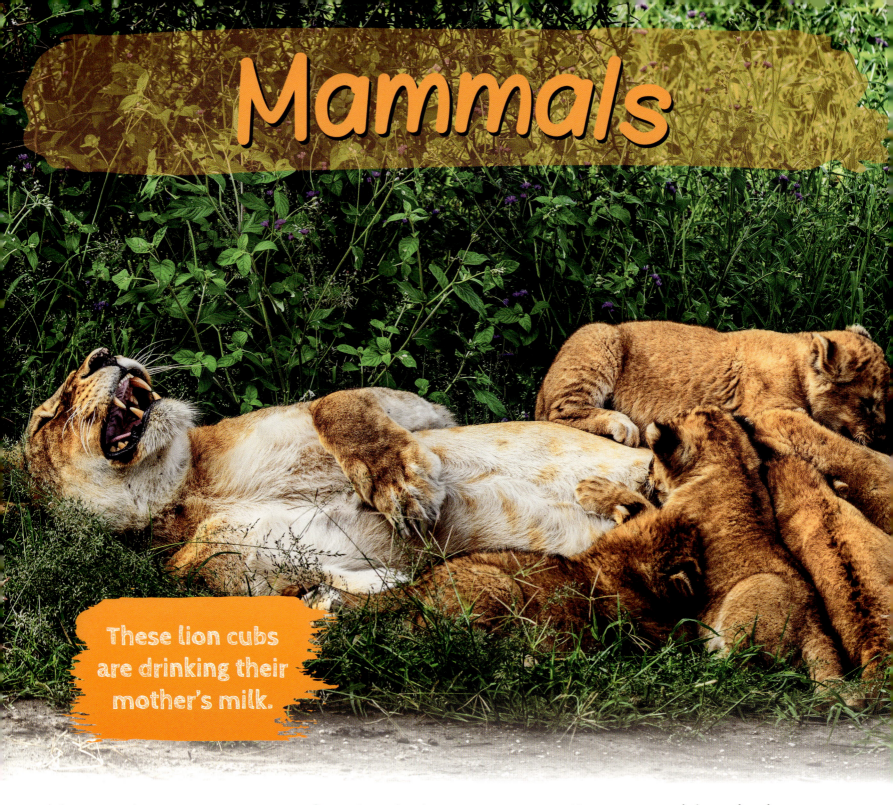

These lion cubs are drinking their mother's milk.

Mammals are a type of animal that are usually **warm-blooded**, have hair or fur and feed their **young** with milk from their bodies. A mammal's young will begin to eat other food as it grows older.

Mammals can be herbivores, carnivores or omnivores.

Some mammals, such as wolves, are carnivores.

Some mammals, such as giraffes, are herbivores.

Some mammals, such as pigs, are omnivores.

Birds

Scarecrows are used to frighten birds away from **crops**.

Many birds are omnivores; they eat seeds, berries and insects. This can cause problems for farmers who have to find ways of protecting their crops from birds.

Birds' beaks are all different. Gouldian finches have short, cone-shaped beaks perfect for picking up seeds. Other birds, like the sword-billed hummingbird, have very long, pointy beaks for eating **nectar** from flowers.

Differences in animals that help them do things like find food are called adaptations.

Gouldian Finch

Sword-Billed Hummingbird

Fish

Great White Shark

Fish can be omnivores, herbivores or carnivores. Most carnivorous animals are also predators. This means they hunt other animals. Great white sharks are one of the ocean's greatest predators.

Great white sharks eat sea lions, seals, sea turtles and even some whales. They will sneak up on their **prey** by swimming underneath them and then attacking from below.

Great whites have adaptations that make them good predators. For example, they have lots of very sharp teeth!

Reptiles

Reptiles are **cold-blooded** animals with scales. Snakes are a type of reptile that hunt other animals for food. Snakes kill their prey by crushing them, or biting them and injecting a **toxin**.

Boa constrictors crush their prey.

After killing an animal, snakes will try to swallow it whole. Most snakes have **jaws** that are adapted to do this and can stretch open really wide.

Amphibians

Salamander

Like many reptiles, amphibians usually swallow their prey whole. Amphibians are also cold-blooded, but unlike reptiles they can breathe on land and underwater. Frogs and salamanders are amphibians.

A frog's tongue is about a third of the length of its body.

Frogs mostly eat insects because they are carnivores. They eat flies, mosquitos, moths and even grasshoppers and worms. Frogs have long, sticky tongues for catching flies while they are mid-flight!

Insects

There are millions of types of insects in the world and they are all very different. Assassin bugs are carnivores. They eat other bugs like bees, flies and caterpillars.

Assassin Bug with Prey

Proboscis

They use a straw-like mouth part, called a proboscis (say: pro-bo-sis), to stab their prey and inject a toxin that turns their insides to mush. They then suck the insect's insides up through the proboscis!

Plants

Plants are able to make their own food from sunlight in a process called photosynthesis (say: fo-toe-sinth-eh-sis). The energy from sunlight is taken in by a green **chemical** in a plant's leaves called chlorophyll (say: clor-uh-fill).

Plants take in carbon dioxide through tiny holes called stomata.

Plants also take in a gas called carbon dioxide from the air. The Sun's energy and the carbon dioxide help to make a type of sugar called glucose which provides food for the plant.

Humans

Humans eat lots of different food, including fruit, vegetables, grains, and animal products such as meat, milk and eggs. People who are vegetarian choose not to eat meat, and people who are vegan don't eat any animal products at all.

It is important for humans to eat a balanced diet. This means eating all types of food. Some foods, such as fruit and vegetables, should be eaten more often than other foods, such as sugary snacks.

Vegans and vegetarians can still eat
a balanced diet too.

Glossary

chemical	substances that materials are made from
cold-blooded	animals that have blood that changes with the temperature around them
crops	plants that are grown on a large scale because they are useful, usually as food
jaws	the upper and lower parts of the mouth containing the teeth
nectar	a sweet liquid made by flowers in order to attract insects
prey	animals that are hunted by other animals for food
processes	a series of activities or natural changes
toxin	a poison produced by a living thing
warm-blooded	animals that have blood that stays at a certain temperature
young	an animal's offspring or babies

Index